WINNERS'
Reading & Writing
5

Clue & Key

WINNERS' Reading & Writing 5

Scope & Sequence

Chapter		Unit	Topic		Reading
1	**Gadgets**	01	Personal Electronic Items	fiction	A Garage Sale
		02	Kitchen Appliances	nonfiction	Technology in Our Kitch
2	**Eating**	03	Foods in Restaurants	fiction	A Night at a Restaura
		04	Global Traditional Foods	nonfiction	Special Foods for Your Travels
3	**Various Characters**	05	Story Characters	fiction	A Party at the Castl
		06	Movie Characters	nonfiction	Famous Movie Characters
4	**People**	07	Describing People	fiction	A Greedy King
		08	Great People	nonfiction	George Washington
5	**Plants**	09	Various Flowers	fiction	In the Garden
		10	Various Trees	nonfiction	Unique Trees
6	**Movies**	11	Opinions about Movies	fiction	An Interview with So Movie Fans
		12	Movie World	nonfiction	A Message from Ray Sa

Language Point	Writing	Writing Point
possessive pronouns	Writing a Report About My Friends' Lost Items	Possessive Adjectives & Possessive Pronouns
be able to	Writing an Advertisement for a New Machine	
some / any	Writing a Restaurant Review	Commas (1)
first conditional	Writing a Letter to My Friend	
comparatives	Writing a Book Report About Some Story Characters	Commas (2)
verb + -ing	Writing a Fan Letter to a Movie Character	
superlatives	Writing a Report on a Survey About My Classmates	Superlatives
when + past tense	Writing an Essay About a Great Person	
be + p.p.	Writing a Play About Flowers	Past Participles
prepositional verbs in the passive	Writing a Report About Trees	
because	Writing a Movie Review	Future Tense
be going to	Completing an Interview Paper	

How to Use
WINNERS' Reading & Writing 5

Student Book

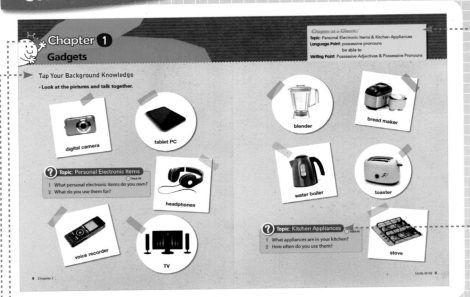

Chapters

In the *WINNERS' Reading & Writing* Series, each book contains six big themes which are all divided into two topics. By reading and writing about a broad range of topics, students can obtain both thematic knowledge and language skills.

Tap Your Background Knowledge

This section introduces basic vocabulary items related to the following two topics. By checking the basic words and corresponding pictures, students can learn new words and build their background knowledge of the topic at the same time. These words will also be a great help when students need additional vocabulary while doing the *Read & Write* section.

Chapter at a Glance

Each chapter begins with a list of learning objectives so that teachers and students can preview the topics and language points presented in the chapter.

Topic Questions

Questions about each topic help students preview each unit and build some background knowledge. By asking and answering questions together, both teachers and students can start the lesson in a relaxing and communicative way.

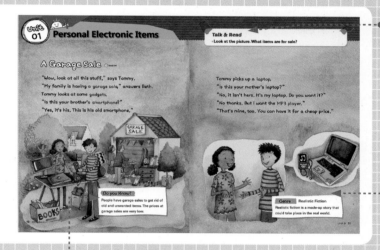

Talk & Read

Before reading, students can preview the story and predict what will happen while talking about the picture.

Each chapter presents a fiction and a nonfiction story, which provide students with a good balance at an early stage of reading.

Genre

By studying the characteristics of each genre, students can better understand the text and become successful in writing in different genres.

Do You Know?

This section gives more information about the topic to the students.

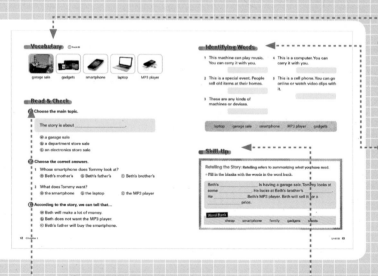

Vocabulary

Each unit introduces five new words from the main story in a format of a picture dictionary.

Identifying Words

Students reinforce their understanding of five target words through this word definition quiz.

Read & Check

The set of comprehension questions that cover topics from finding the main idea to checking detailed information helps students fully understand the story.

Skill-Up

Through this section, students can learn and practice essential reading skills to become effective and independent readers.

You can download the MP3 files for this book at
www.clueandkey.com

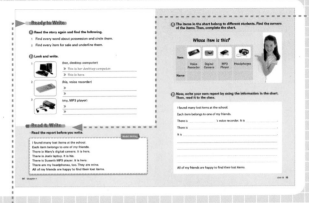

Read & Write

The writing section begins with a model writing which shows the goal of the writing task.

The topic and the model writing are given, but students can still choose their own interests or personalized contents for their writing. They can use the vocabulary and language point they learned, which enables teachers to check students' overall understanding of each unit.

As students complete writing tasks in different genres or text types, they will be able to gain a lot of confidence and interest in writing. Feedback from peers will result in a more fun and productive writing lesson.

Ready to Write

After reading and understanding the story, students can use this section to find and recognize the main language point (the target grammar) in the story by themselves.

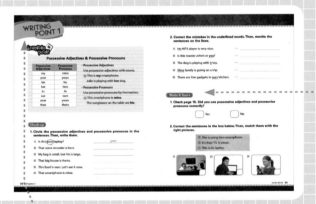

Make It Yours

This section enables students to apply what they have learned to their own writing. Students should be encouraged to refer back to the sentences they wrote and to check for mistakes by themselves. This proofreading and editing practice will lead students to become better writers and readers.

Writing Point

Each chapter ends with a special section for building writing accuracy with grammar and punctuation exercises.

Workbook

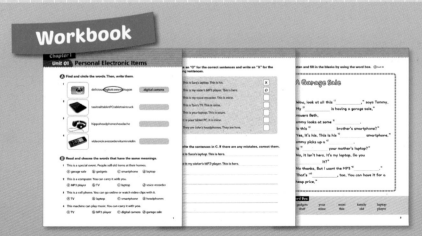

Workbook

By wrapping up the lesson through these exercises, students can reinforce their vocabulary, grammar, and listening skills.

CONTENTS

Chapter 1 8

Unit 01	Personal Electronic Items	10
Unit 02	Kitchen Appliances	16
WRITING POINT 1		22

Chapter 2 24

Unit 03	Foods in Restaurants	26
Unit 04	Global Traditional Foods	32
WRITING POINT 2		38

Chapter 3 40

Unit 05	Story Characters	42
Unit 06	Movie Characters	48
WRITING POINT 3		54

Chapter 4 56

Unit 07	Describing People	58
Unit 08	Great People	64
WRITING POINT 4		70

Chapter 5 72

Unit 09	Flowers	74
Unit 10	Trees	80
WRITING POINT 5		86

Chapter 6 88

Unit 11	Opinions about Movies	90
Unit 12	Movie World	96
WRITING POINT 6		102

Chapter 1

Gadgets

Tap Your Background Knowledge

■ **Look at the pictures and talk together.**

digital camera

tablet PC

? Topic: Personal Electronic Items

Track 02

1 What personal electronic items do you own?
2 What do you use them for?

headphones

voice recorder

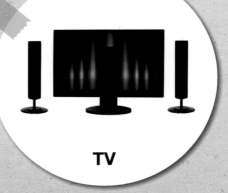

TV

Chapter at a Glance

Topic: Personal Electronic Items & Kitchen Appliances
Language Point: possessive pronouns
                    be able to
Writing Point: Possessive Adjectives & Possessive Pronouns

blender

bread maker

water boiler

toaster

stove

? **Topic**: Kitchen Appliances

Track 03

1   What appliances are in your kitchen?
2   How often do you use them?

Personal Electronic Items

A Garage Sale ◎ Track 04

"Wow, look at all this stuff," says Tommy.

"My family is having a garage sale," answers Beth.

Tommy looks at some gadgets.

"Is this your brother's smartphone?"

"Yes, it's his. This is his old smartphone."

Do you Know?

People have garage sales to get rid of old and unwanted items. The prices at garage sales are very low.

Talk & Read

▪ **Look at the picture. What items are for sale?**

Tommy picks up a laptop.

"Is this your mother's laptop?"

"No, it isn't hers. It's my laptop. Do you want it?"

"No thanks. But I want the MP3 player."

"That's mine, too. You can have it for a cheap price."

Genre Realistic Fiction

Realistic fiction is a made-up story that could take place in the real world.

Vocabulary

garage sale

gadgets

smartphone

laptop

MP3 player

Read & Check

A **Choose the main topic.**

The story is about _____.

ⓐ a garage sale

ⓑ a department store sale

ⓒ an electronics store sale

B **Choose the correct answers.**

1 Whose smartphone does Tommy look at?
   ⓐ Beth's mother's   ⓑ Beth's father's   ⓒ Beth's brother's

2 What does Tommy want?
   ⓐ the smartphone   ⓑ the laptop   ⓒ the MP3 player

C **According to the story, we can tell that...**

ⓐ Beth will make a lot of money.

ⓑ Beth does not want the MP3 player.

ⓒ Beth's father will buy the smartphone.

Identifying Words

1 This machine can play music. You can carry it with you.

2 This is a special event. People sell old items at their homes.

3 These are any kinds of machines or devices.

4 This is a computer. You can carry it with you.

5 This is a cell phone. You can go online or watch video clips with it.

laptop   garage sale   smartphone   MP3 player   gadgets

Skill-Up

Retelling the Story: Retelling refers to summarizing what you have read.

✫ Fill in the blanks with the words in the word bank.

Beth's _____ is having a garage sale. Tommy looks at some _____. He looks at Beth's brother's _____. He _____ Beth's MP3 player. Beth will sell it for a _____ price.

Word Bank

cheap   smartphone   family   gadgets   wants

A Read the story again and find the following.

1 Find every word about possession and circle them.

2 Find every item for sale and underline them.

B Look and write.

1  (her, desktop computer)

>> This is her desktop computer.

>> This is hers.

2 (his, voice recorder)

>>

>>

3 (my, MP3 player)

>>

>>

Read & Write

- Read the report before you write.

I found many lost items at the school.
Each item belongs to one of my friends.
There is Mary's digital camera. It is hers.
There is Joe's laptop. It is his.
There is Susan's MP3 player. It is hers.
There are my headphones, too. They are mine.
All of my friends are happy to find their lost items.

A The items in the chart belong to different students. Find the owners of the items. Then, complete the chart.

Whose item is this?

Item	Voice Recorder	Digital Camera	MP3 Player	Headphones
Name				

B Now, write your own report by using the information in the chart. Then, read it to the class.

I found many lost items at the school.

Each item belongs to one of my friends.

There is _____'s voice recorder. It is _____.

There is _____.

It is _____.

_____

_____

_____

_____

All of my friends are happy to find their lost items.

Kitchen Appliances

Technology in Our Kitchens

Track 06

The modern kitchen has many machines.

They are useful to people.

Most kitchens have a refrigerator.

We are able to keep food cold in it.

Do you Know?

Most refrigerators have a special section called a freezer. We put items such as ice cream and ice cubes here to keep them frozen.

Talk & Read

- Look at the picture. How does the kitchen look?

Most kitchens have a microwave and a blender, too.

People are able to cook food quickly in a microwave.

People are able to chop food with a blender.

Some kitchens have a toaster.

We are able to make toast with a toaster.

They make cooking very easy.

Genre　Magazine Article

A magazine article is usually short. It provides information about a certain topic.

Vocabulary Track 07

| modern | refrigerator | microwave | chop | toast |

Read & Check

A Choose the main topic.

The story is about _____.

ⓐ how to cook a good meal
ⓑ useful kitchen appliances
ⓒ people's favorite kitchen appliances

B Choose the correct answers.

1 What keeps food cold?
   ⓐ a toaster   ⓑ a refrigerator   ⓒ a microwave

2 What can people do with a microwave?
   ⓐ cook food quickly   ⓑ chop food quickly   ⓒ mix food quickly

C According to the passage, we can tell that...

ⓐ a blender can make toast.
ⓑ not every kitchen has a toaster.
ⓒ people keep food in a microwave.

Identifying Words

1 This is cooked bread.

2 This cooks food quickly.

3 This keeps food cold.

4 This is the opposite of "old."

5 This means "to cut something into small pieces."

microwave   chop   modern   toast   refrigerator

Skill-Up

Similarities and Differences: It is essential to think about how the subjects are alike and different.

✯ Read the passage again and find the similarities and differences between a blender, a microwave, a toaster, and a refrigerator.

Similarities

1

2

3

Differences

4 Blender

5 Microwave

6 Toaster

7 Refrigerator

ⓐ It makes toast.

ⓑ It makes cooking very easy.

ⓒ It is used in modern kitchens.

ⓓ It chops food.

ⓔ It cooks food quickly.

ⓕ It keeps food cold.

ⓖ It is very useful to people.

Ready to Write

A **Read the passage again and find the following.**

1 Find every "are able to" and circle them.

2 Find every kitchen appliance and underline them.

B **Look and write.**

1  (freeze food, freezer)

   >> *People are able to freeze food with a freezer.*

2  (make bread, bread maker)

   >>

3  (cook food, stove)

   >>

Read & Write

- **Read the advertisement before you write.**

Buy the Blender-Toaster 2000 today!

The Blender-Toaster 2000 is a new invention.
You are able to chop food into small pieces with it.
So you are able to prepare food for dinner easily.
You are able to make toast with it, too.
The Blender-Toaster 2000 is perfect for your kitchen.
Order now!

A Look at the pictures. Combine two of the kitchen appliances into one machine. Then, draw it. What can your new machine do?

blender   toaster   bread maker

stove   microwave   water boiler

B Now, write an advertisement for your new machine. Then, read it to the class.

Buy the _____ **today!**
    (The name of your new machine)

The _____ is a new invention.

You are able to _____.

You _____.

_____

_____

_____

The _____ is perfect for your kitchen.

Order now!

Possessive Adjectives & Possessive Pronouns

Possessive Adjectives	Possessive Pronouns
my	mine
your	yours
his	his
her	hers
its	its
our	ours
your	yours
their	theirs

- **Possessive Adjectives**

  Use possessive adjectives with nouns.

  ex This is **my** smartphone.

  Julie is playing with **her** dog.

- **Possessive Pronouns**

  Use possessive pronouns by themselves.

  ex This smartphone is **mine**.

  The sunglasses on the table are **his**.

Check-up

1. Circle the possessive adjectives and possessive pronouns in the sentences. Then, write them.

1) Is this your laptop? _____ your

2) That voice recorder is hers. _____

3) My bag is small, but his is large. _____

4) That big house is theirs. _____

5) This food is ours. Let's eat it now. _____

6) That smartphone is mine. _____

2. Correct the mistakes in the underlined words. Then, rewrite the sentences on the lines.

1) <u>He</u> MP3 player is very nice. ····▸ _____

2) Is this toaster John's or <u>you</u>? ····▸ _____

3) The dog is playing with <u>it</u> toy. ····▸ _____

4) <u>Mine</u> family is going on a trip. ····▸ _____

5) There are five gadgets in <u>ours</u> kitchen. ····▸ _____

Make It Yours

1. Check page 15. Did you use possessive adjectives and possessive pronouns correctly?

☐ Yes ☐ No

2. Correct the sentences in the box below. Then, match them with the right pictures.

ⓐ She is using hers smartphone.

ⓑ It's their TV. It's their.

ⓒ This is he laptop.

1)

2)

3)

Chapter 2
Eating

Tap Your Background Knowledge

■ **Look at the pictures and talk together.**

appetizer

soup

◎ Track 08

? **Topic:** Foods in Restaurants

1 What is your favorite restaurant?
2 What food do you usually eat there?

main dish

dessert

salad

Chapter at a Glance

Topic: Foods in Restaurants & Global Traditional Foods
Language Point: some / any
first conditional
Writing Point: Commas (1)

sushi

fish and chips

paella

lasagna

? Topic: Global Traditional Foods

Track 09

1 What are some traditional foods in your country?

2 How do you like those foods?

curry and naan

Foods in Restaurants

A Night at a Restaurant ⊙ Track 10

⟨Setting⟩

A boy and a girl are having dinner in a restaurant.

Waiter : May I take your order, please?

Molly : Do you have any salads?

Waiter : Yes, we have some salads.

Steve : Do you have any appetizers?

Waiter : Sorry. We don't have any appetizers.

Today's special is pasta. Do you want some?

Do you Know?

You can find the special of the day on most restaurant menus. It means that the chef especially recommends that dish. Sometimes it is cheaper than the normal price.

Talk & Read

- **Look at the picture. What are the children doing?**

Steve : Okay. I'll have some pasta, please.

Waiter : How about you, miss?

Do you want some pasta, too?

Molly : [Thinking for a while] No thanks.

I want some salads and seafood.

Waiter : Sure. Anything to drink?

Molly : We'd like some iced tea, please.

Genre Play

A play is a story that people can act by saying lines while they perform.

Vocabulary

restaurant

waiter

order

pasta

iced tea

Read & Check

A Choose the main topic.

The story is about _____.

ⓐ a new restaurant

ⓑ ordering at a restaurant

ⓒ Molly and Steve's restaurant

B Choose the correct answers.

1 What does Steve order?

ⓐ pizza　　　　ⓑ seafood　　　　ⓒ pasta

2 What does Molly order to drink?

ⓐ juice　　　　ⓑ iced tea　　　　ⓒ water

C According to the story, we can tell that...

ⓐ the waiter is Steve's friend.

ⓑ Molly always orders salads.

ⓒ the restaurant does not have all kinds of foods.

Identifying Words

1 This is cold tea. It is usually served with ice.

4 You can order food and eat at this place.

2 This food tastes like spaghetti. It has various shapes.

5 This person serves you at a restaurant.

3 This is something you do at a restaurant to get food. You usually tell this to the waiter.

order   waiter   iced tea   restaurant   pasta

Skill-Up

Knowing About Setting, the Characters, and Plot:
The setting is the time (when) and place (where) in a story. The characters are the people or others in a story, and the plot is the main events in a story.

✫ Read the story again and find the answers.

When	+	Where	+	Characters

⟨ **The Food They Order** ⟩

Steve	**Molly**
Asks About: _____	Asks About: _____
Orders: _____ and _____	Orders: _____ and _____

Ready to Write

A **Read the story again and find the following.**

1 Find every "some" and "any" and circle them.

2 Find every type of food and underline them.

B **Look and write.**

1  (have, side dishes)

>> *We have some side dishes.*

_____

2  (don't have, desserts)

>>

_____

3 (have, salads)

>>

_____

Read & Write

■ **Read the restaurant review before you write.**

Name of the Restaurant: Primo's
Location: 243 Checketts St. Ranmoor, Sheffield
Rating: ★★★★☆

Primo's is a new Italian restaurant downtown.
It has some good pasta and seafood.
It also has great appetizers.
But it doesn't have any desserts.
Overall, *Primo's* is a very good restaurant. I recommend it.

A **Choose and write three foods for your restaurant. Then, ask your friend what his or her restaurant has. Write the names of the foods on the dishes.**

My Restaurant

Name:

My Friend's Restaurant

Name:

iced tea   soup   dessert   appetizer   pasta   salad

B **Now, write a restaurant review about your friend's restaurant. Then, read it to the class.**

Name of the Restaurant: _____

Location: _____

Rating: ☆☆☆☆☆

_____ is a new restaurant downtown.

It has some _____.

It also has _____.

_____

But it doesn't have any _____.

_____

_____

Global Traditional Foods

Special Foods for Your Travels

Track 12

There are a lot of traditional foods in every country.

If you visit Thailand, you should eat pad Thai.

If you travel to Japan, you should eat sushi and ramen.

You will love the noodles.

Do you Know?

Many countries' traditional foods use special kinds of ingredients. Thai food includes lots of seafood. Italian food uses lots of pasta. And Chinese food uses lots of rice.

■ Look at the pictures. Did you try any foods in the pictures?

If you go to Mexico, you should have tacos and salsa.

Tacos and salsa are spicy but delicious.

If you visit England, you should try fish and chips.

If you go to Spain, you should have paella.

These foods will make your travels very special.

Genre Magazine Article

A magazine article is usually short. It provides information about a certain topic.

Vocabulary Track 13

pad Thai

travel

noodles

taco

delicious

Read & Check

Ⓐ Choose the main topic.

The story is about _____.

ⓐ a special meal

ⓑ traditional foods

ⓒ a trip around the world

Ⓑ Choose the correct answers.

1 What should people eat in Thailand?

   ⓐ sushi   ⓑ pad Thai   ⓒ ramen

2 How do tacos and salsa taste?

   ⓐ spicy   ⓑ sweet   ⓒ sour

Ⓒ According to the passage, we can tell that...

ⓐ Thai food uses seafood.

ⓑ people only eat fish in England.

ⓒ noodles are a traditional food in Japan.

1 This is another word for "tasty."

2 This means "to take a trip."

3 This is a traditional food in Thailand.

4 This is a type of food like spaghetti and ramen.

5 This is a Mexican food with meat, cheese, vegetables, and sauce in a hard shell.

travel   pad Thai   noodles   delicious   taco

Skill-Up

Classifying: Classifying means putting things that are related into groups.

☆ Read the passage again. Then, complete the chart.

	Countries	Traditional Foods
	Thailand	pad Thai

Ready to Write

A **Read the passage again and find the following.**

1 Find every "if" and circle them.

2 Find every type of food and underline them.

B **Look and write.**

1

(Russia, stuffed cabbage)

» *If you go to Russia, you should have stuffed cabbage.*

2

(India, curry and naan)

»

3

(Italy, lasagna)

»

Read & Write

▪ **Read the letter before you write.**

Dear Katie,
I heard about your trip around the world.
There are many foods you should try.
If you visit China, you should have dim sum.
If you visit Italy, you should have pizza.
Have a great trip.

Your friend,
Justin

A Look at the food from each country. Which foods do you want your friend to try? Circle three of the foods.

sushi / Japan   curry and naan / India   fish and chips / England

paella / Spain   baklava / Turkey   dim sum / China

B Now, write a letter. Then, read it to the class.

Dear _____ ,

I heard about your trip around the world.

There are many foods you should try.

If you visit _____ , you should have _____ .

If _____ .

_____

_____

_____

Your friend,

_____

WRITING POINT 2

Commas (1)

• Use a comma when the if-clause is at the beginning of the sentence.

| , |

ex **If** you are hungry**,** eat some food.

   If we visit Thailand**,** we will have pad Thai.

• Do not use a comma when the if-clause is in the middle of the sentence.

ex You will enjoy the food **if** you eat it.

   We will order pizza **if** we go to the restaurant.

Check-up

1. Circle "if" in each sentence. Then, add a comma where needed.

1) If you are ready I will take your order.

2) We will visit London if we go to England.

3) There will be no time if you wake up late.

4) If it is raining bring an umbrella.

5) Do you want anything if we order some food?

6) If I go to Europe I will travel by train.

2. Rewrite the sentences on the lines. Put "if" in the correct place in each sentence.

1) You have salads, I want to have one. ····▸ _____

2) You should have dim sum you visit China. ····▸ _____

3) We can take a break you are tired. ····▸ _____

4) You are hungry, you should try the pasta. ····▸ _____

5) You go to Japan, eat some sushi. ····▸ _____

Make It Yours

1. Check page 37. Did you use "if" and commas correctly?

◻ Yes   ◻ No

2. Correct the sentences in the box below. Then, match them with the right pictures.

ⓐ You go to Mexico, you should have tacos.

ⓑ If you visit Thailand you should eat pad Thai.

ⓒ You should have paella you go to Spain.

1)    2)    3)

Chapter 3
Various Characters

Tap Your Background Knowledge

▪ **Look at the pictures and talk together.**

Goldilocks

Cinderella

? Topic: Story Characters

Track 14

1 Which story characters do you know?
2 How do you like these characters?

Aladdin

The Three Little Pigs

Pinocchio

Chapter at a Glance

Topic: Story Characters & Movie Characters
Language Point: comparatives
[verb + -ing]
Writing Point: Commas (2)

Woody

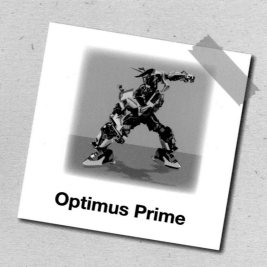

Optimus Prime

Batman

Superman

Captain Jack Sparrow

? **Topic**: Movie Characters

○ Track 15

1 Which movie characters do you know?
2 What do you think of them?

Story Characters

A Party at the Castle ◎ Track 16

Some fairy tale women are having a party at the castle.

"I'm more active than you. I can swim everywhere,"
says the Little Mermaid.

"But I'm more intelligent than you," answers Gretel.

"I tricked the evil witch."

Do you Know?

Some of the most popular fairy tales
are *Cinderella*, *Sleeping Beauty*, and
The Three Little Pigs.

Talk & Read

- Look at the picture. Which story characters are at the party?

"I'm more popular," says Snow White.

"Prince Charming loves me."

"But my clothes are more expensive than yours,"
says Little Red Riding Hood.

"Look at my nice red clothes."

"I'm sleepier than everyone," says Sleeping Beauty.

"I'm going to bed now."

Genre Fantasy

Fantasy is a type of make-believe story. It is often set in an unreal world.

Vocabulary

◉ Track 17

| castle | active | intelligent | witch | popular |

Read & Check

Ⓐ Choose the main topic.

The story is about _____.

ⓐ a group of princesses

ⓑ the prince's new castle

ⓒ some story characters at a party

Ⓑ Choose the correct answers.

1   Where are the fairy tale women?

ⓐ at a house   ⓑ at a castle   ⓒ in a park

2   Who tricked the evil witch?

ⓐ Gretel   ⓑ Snow White   ⓒ Cinderella

Ⓒ According to the story, we can tell that…

ⓐ Gretel thinks she is smart.

ⓑ Prince Charming is at the party.

ⓒ the castle is Snow White's home.

Identifying Words

1 This is a woman. She can use bad magic.

2 This is another word for "smart."

3 This means "well-liked."

4 This means "busy and energetic."

5 This is a large building with high walls around it. A king or queen may live here.

| intelligent | active | popular | witch | castle |

Skill-Up

Describing the Characters: Describing characters means giving detailed information about what they are like.

☆ Read the story again. Then, complete the chart.

	Character	What the Character Is Like	The Reason
1	The Little Mermaid	active	She can swim everywhere.
2			
3			
4			

Ready to Write

A **Read the story again and find the following.**

1 Find every "more" and circle them.

2 Find every adjective after "more" and underline them.

B **Look and write.**

1

(handsome, Pinocchio)

» I am more handsome than Pinocchio.

2

(intelligent, Aladdin)

»

3

(popular, Little Mermaid)

»

Read & Write

▪ **Read the book report before you write.**

Model Writing

I read some story books yesterday.

I want to compare some of the story characters.

First, I think Gretel is more intelligent than the Little Mermaid.

Gretel tricked the evil witch.

Second, Cinderella is more beautiful than Little Red Riding Hood.

She is very tall and pretty.

But I think they are all great and fun characters.

A Look at the picture. What is each character like? Choose the characters and adjectives you want to use.

Pinocchio

Little Red Riding Hood

Snow White

Goldilocks

Sleeping Beauty

Aladdin

active   friendly   handsome   beautiful   intelligent   popular

B Now, write a report. Then, read it to the class.

I read some story books yesterday.

I want to compare some of the story characters.

First, I think _____ is more _____ than

_____.

_____

Second, _____.

_____

Third, _____.

_____

_____

Unit 06

Movie Characters

Famous Movie Characters ⊙ Track 18

by Carla Waters

There are many famous movie characters.

Shrek is a scary-looking ogre.

Ogres are imaginary monsters. They like fighting.

But Shrek enjoys living a peaceful life.

Panda Po in *Kung Fu Panda* is an animal character.

Pandas are usually slow and lazy.

But Panda Po is very energetic.

He enjoys doing kung fu.

Do you Know?

There are many movie genres. Some of them are animation, action, adventure, horror, and drama.

Talk & Read

- **Look at the pictures. Which movie characters do you see?**

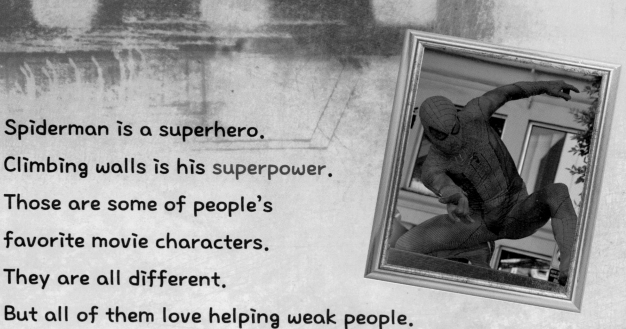

Spiderman is a superhero.

Climbing walls is his superpower.

Those are some of people's

favorite movie characters.

They are all different.

But all of them love helping weak people.

Genre Report

A report is a paper for school. Students write reports to provide information about certain topics.

Vocabulary

scary-looking

imaginary

peaceful

lazy

superpower

Read & Check

Ⓐ Choose the main topic.

The story is about _____.

ⓐ going to see a movie

ⓑ different kinds of movies

ⓒ favorite movie characters

Ⓑ Choose the correct answers.

1 What is Panda Po like?

ⓐ He is energetic.   ⓑ He is scary.   ⓒ He is gentle.

2 What is Spiderman's special power?

ⓐ climbing walls   ⓑ super strength   ⓒ flying

Ⓒ According to the passage, we can tell that...

ⓐ Panda Po is a real panda.

ⓑ Spiderman is a bad person.

ⓒ some people are afraid of Shrek.

Identifying Words

1 This is a superhero's ability such as flying in the sky.

4 This is the opposite of "actual" or "real."

2 This means "quiet and restful."

5 This means "slow to move and react."

3 This means something looks frightening.

peaceful   imaginary   scary-looking   superpower   lazy

Skill-Up

Similarities and Differences: It is essential to think about how the subjects are alike and different.

☆ Read the passage again and find the similarities and differences between the Shrek, Panda Po, and Spiderman.

Similarities

1

2

Differences

3 Shrek

4 Panda Po

5 Spiderman

ⓐ He has a superpower.

ⓑ He is an animal character.

ⓒ He is a very popular movie character.

ⓓ He likes helping people.

ⓔ He likes a peaceful life.

Ready to Write

A **Read the passage again and find the following.**

1 Find every word that ends with "-ing" and circle them.

2 Find every word that describes the movie characters and underline them.

B **Look and write.**

1
(Superman, like, fly in the sky)

>> Superman likes flying in the sky.

2
(Optimus Prime, enjoy, change into a truck)

>>

3
(Shrek, like, help others)

>>

Read & Write

Read the fan letter before you write.

Dear Hermione,

You are my favorite character in the *Harry Potter* movies.
You are so clever and intelligent. You enjoy solving difficult problems.
You are also very kind. You like helping people in trouble.
I like helping people, too. I want to be more like you.

Your fan,
Julie

A Look at the movie characters. Choose your favorite character. What is he or she like?

B Now, write a fan letter to one of the characters. Then, read it to the class.

Dear _____

You are my favorite character in _____.

You are _____.

You enjoy _____.

You are also _____.

_____

_____

_____

_____

Commas (2)

Use commas when you write letters.

,

- **greetings** – Always use a comma after the greeting in a letter.

  ex Dear Spiderman,

  Dear Snow White,

- **closings** – Always use a comma after the closing in a letter.

  ex Your fan,   Your best friend,   Sincerely yours,

  Tom   Julie   Kate

Check-up

1. Read the letter. Add commas after the words that need them.

1)

Dear Spiderman

You are my favorite movie
character.
I think you are the best.
You always catch the bad people.
You help others, too.
You're great.

Your fan
Steve

2)

Dear Woody

I watched *Toy Story* yesterday.
I really like you because you are
very helpful. You enjoy helping
your friends all the time.
I want to be like you.
Take care.

Your biggest fan
Fiona

2. Look at the greetings and closings. Add commas when needed.

1) Dear Shrek

2) Your fan
Amanda

3) Your biggest fan
Crystal

4) Dear Spiderman

5) Dear Little Red Riding Hood

6) Your friend
Daniel

7) Sincerely yours
Trevor

8) Dear Snow White

Make It Yours

1. Check page 53. Did you use commas after the greeting and closing correctly?

☐ Yes   ☐ No

2. Write the a greeting and a closing for each letter. Use commas in the right places.

1)

Jamie → Batman

_____

You're my favorite movie character.
I like you because you are very strong.
I want to meet you one day.

_____
_____

2)

Tom → Superman

_____

I saw you in the movie last night.
I think you fly very well.
You are amazing.
How can you do that?

_____
_____

Chapter 4
People

Tap Your Background Knowledge

- **Look at the pictures and talk together.**

funny

shy

? **Topic:** Describing People

Track 20

1 What are your friends like?
2 What are you like?

strong

mean

smart

Chapter at a Glance

Topic: Describing People & Great People
Language Point: superlatives
 [when + past tense]
Writing Point: Superlatives

Marie Curie
scientist

Jane Austen
writer

Wright Brothers
inventors

Pablo Neruda
poet

? **Topic**: Great People

Track 21

1 How much do you know about these people?

2 Who are some famous people in your country?

Vincent van Gogh
painter

Unit 07

Describing People

A Greedy King ● Track 22

One day, a king announces, "I want the best people."

Two weeks later, many people visit the palace.

"I'm the tallest athlete," says a man.

"I'm the smartest witch," says a woman.

Do you Know?

Some countries around the world still have kings. Thailand, the Netherlands, and Spain all have kings.

Talk & Read

- **Look at the picture. What is each person like?**

"I'm the richest merchant," says another man.

"And I'm the funniest person," says a boy.

The king says, "I'm the happiest king on Earth.

You cannot go back to your homes.

All of you should work for me forever."

"What?" say the people. "You're so greedy. Goodbye."

Genre   Fantasy

Fantasy is a type of make-believe story. The people in the stories can often do magic.

Vocabulary Track 23

palace

athlete

merchant

Earth

greedy

Read & Check

A Choose the main topic.

The story is about _____.

ⓐ rich people

ⓑ a greedy king

ⓒ the smartest woman

B Choose the correct answers.

1 What does the king want?
ⓐ the tallest people   ⓑ the funniest people   ⓒ the best people

2 What do the people call the king?
ⓐ a good king   ⓑ a greedy king   ⓒ a smart king

C According to the story, we can tell that…

ⓐ the boy is smarter than the woman.

ⓑ the people are unhappy with the king.

ⓒ the king lives in a palace with the people.

Identifying Words

1 This person is very good at sports.

2 This is a king's or queen's home.

3 This person buys and sells goods and earns money.

4 This is our planet.

5 This means "having a feeling of wanting more and more."

merchant   palace   greedy   Earth   athlete

Skill-Up

Inference: Inference is drawing conclusions by using the information people say or write.

✫ Match each sentence with the correct inference.

1 The king only wants the best people. •

2 The people say, "You're so greedy," to the king. •

3 The king says, "I'm the happiest king on Earth." •

ⓐ They don't like the king.

ⓑ He is greedy.

ⓒ The king likes all of the best people.

Ready to Write

A **Read the story again and find the following.**

1 Find every word that ends with "-est" and circle them.

2 Find every "I'm the" and underline them.

B **Look and write.**

1

(she, cute, girl)

» She's the cutest girl.

2

(he, greedy, man)

»

3

(she, strong, girl)

»

Read & Write

▪ **Read the survey before you write.**

There are many students at King Elementary School.
The students are all different from each other.
Sally has the longest hair.
Greg is the funniest boy.
Mario has the shortest hair.
Angela is the smartest girl.
And Ryan has the biggest feet.

A Talk to your friends and fill in the blanks. Then, write about them.

Find someone who...

name

has the longest fingers

has the shortest hair

has the biggest feet

has the longest hair

is the tallest

is the funniest

is the shortest

is the smartest

B Now, write a report on your own survey. Then, read it to the class.

There are many students at _____ School.

The students are all different from each other.

_____ has the _____.

_____ is the _____.

_____ has _____.

_____ is _____.

_____

_____

_____

And _____.

Great People

George Washington ⊙ Track 24

George Washington was a great man in American history.

He grew up in Virginia.

He was an honest and hardworking child.

When he was 21, he joined the army.

When he was 27, he got married.

His wife was Martha Custis.

Do you Know?

George Washington is one of the most famous Americans. Americans call him "Father of His Country."

- Look at the pictures. Do you know who he is?

When he was 43, he became a general in the army.
When he was 57, he became the first president of the United States.
In 1799, he died, but a lot of people still remember him.

Genre Biography

A biography is a true story about a person's life. The person is usually famous.

Vocabulary

hardworking

wife

general

president

remember

Read & Check

A **Choose the main topic.**

The story is about _____.

ⓐ the life of George Washington

ⓑ the wife of George Washington

ⓒ the family of George Washington

B **Choose the correct answers.**

1 What kind of child was George Washington?

ⓐ lazy   ⓑ silly   ⓒ honest

2 What did George Washington NOT do?

ⓐ get married   ⓑ write a book   ⓒ become a general

C **According to the passage, we can tell that...**

ⓐ George Washington was a famous man.

ⓑ George Washington had many children.

ⓒ George Washington always lived in Virginia.

Identifying Words

1 This is the opposite of "lazy."

2 This is the leader of a country.

3 This is a woman. She is married to her husband.

4 This is the leader of an army.

5 This is the opposite of "to forget."

president   remember   hardworking   general   wife

Skill-Up

Sequencing Events: Sequencing events means putting activities in order from the beginning to the end.

☆ Read the passage again. Then, put the events in the correct order.

- George Washington became a general in the army.
- George Washington got married.
- George Washington became the president of the United States.
- George Washington died.
- George Washington joined the army.
- George Washington grew up in Virginia.

Ready to Write

A **Read the passage again and find the following.**

1 Find every "when" and circle them.

2 Find every age and underline them.

B **Look and write.**

1

(he, 25, travel around the world)

>> When he was 25, he traveled around the world.

2

(he, 55, become the president)

>>

3

(she, 29, get married)

>>

Read & Write

Read the essay before you write.

Model Writing

William Shakespeare was born in 1564.
When he was 18, he got married.
When he was 21, he moved to London.
When he was 25, he wrote his first play.
Shakespeare wrote more than 30 plays in his life.
In 1616, Shakespeare died.
But many people say he is the greatest writer in history.

A **Draw and complete the information about a great person in your country.**

The Life of ___Abraham Lincoln___

Year	Age	What He Did
1809		born
1831	22	study law
1842	33	get married to Mary Todd
1861	52	become president of the U.S.
1865	56	die

The Life of _____

Year	Age	What He / She Did

B **Now, write your own essay. Then, read it to the class.**

_____ was born in _____ .

When _____ .

_____

_____

_____

_____

_____

Superlatives

- Make superlative adjectives by adding **-est** to the ends of adjectives. Then, use **the** in front of the adjectives. Some adjectives end with **-y**. For them, change **-y** to **-i**. Then, add **-est** to the end.

  ex fast - the fastest   happy - the happiest

  slow - the slowest   silly - the silliest

  short - the shortest   funny - the funniest

- For some adjectives, double the last consonant, and then add **-est** to the end.

  ex big - the biggest   thin - the thinnest

  fat - the fattest   sad - the saddest

Check-up

1. Circle the superlative adjectives in the sentences. Then, write them on the lines.

1) Jane is the nicest woman. _____

2) George Washington was the greatest president. _____

3) Who is the funniest person? _____

4) That is the smallest animal. _____

5) The baby is the youngest person in the room. _____

6) Patty is the happiest girl in my class. _____

7) Sloth is the slowest animal. _____

2. Correct the mistakes in the underlined words. Then, rewrite the sentences on the lines.

1) He is the <u>greedyest</u> king in the world. ····▶ _____

2) Steve is the <u>fatest</u> man in the city. ····▶ _____

3) Who is the <u>funnyest</u> person you know? ····▶ _____

4) The snail is the <u>slowst</u> animal. ····▶ _____

5) They are the <u>happyst</u> couple. ····▶ _____

Make It Yours

1. Check page 63. Did you use superlative adjectives correctly?

Yes ☐   No ☐

2. Correct the sentences in the box below. Then, match them with the right pictures.

ⓐ He is the smartst boy.

ⓑ Sue is the funnyest girl.

ⓒ Karen has longest hair.

1)

2)

3)

Chapter 5
Plants

Tap Your Background Knowledge

- **Look at the pictures and talk together.**

tulip

lily

? Topic: Various Flowers

⊙ Track 26

1 What is your favorite flower?
2 What does it look like?

daisy

orchid

rose

Chapter at a Glance

Topic: Various Flowers & Various Trees
Language Point: [be + p.p.]
prepositional verbs in the passive
Writing Point: Past Participles

leaves

branches

trunk

fruits

? **Topic**: Various Trees

◉ Track 27

1   What kinds of fruit trees do you know?
2   How do the parts of a tree change
with the seasons?

roots

Flowers

In the Garden ◎ Track 28

Suzie visits her flower garden in the morning.

She goes there to have a great time.

She waters her roses.

She pulls up some weeds around the tulips.

She picks a few daisies, and then she plants

some sunflowers.

Suzie has a wonderful garden.

Do you Know?

Many people have gardens. Roses, tulips, carnations, and lilies are some of the most popular flowers in these gardens.

Talk & Read

▪ Look at the pictures. What flowers are growing in the garden?

The flower garden is visited by Suzie in the morning.

The roses are watered.

Some weeds around the tulips are pulled up.

A few daisies are picked, and then some sunflowers are planted.

What a nice garden Suzie has!

Genre	Realistic Fiction

Realistic fiction is a made-up story about events that could happen in real life.

Vocabulary ⊙ Track 29

flower garden

water

pull up

weed

sunflower

Read & Check

Ⓐ Choose the main topic.

The story is about _____.

ⓐ Suzie and her flower garden

ⓑ the most popular flowers

ⓒ how to start a flower garden

Ⓑ Choose the correct answers.

1 What does Suzie pull up?

ⓐ roses   ⓑ daisies   ⓒ weeds

2 What is picked by Suzie?

ⓐ tulips   ⓑ daisies   ⓒ roses

Ⓒ According to the story, we can tell that...

ⓐ Suzie likes her flower garden.

ⓑ Suzie will plant some more weeds.

ⓒ the roses smell very nice.

Identifying Words

1 This is a tall yellow flower.

2 This means "to give flowers water."

3 This is a bad plant in a flower garden.

4 This is an outdoor place with many flowers.

5 This means "to remove from the ground."

water   flower garden   pull up   sunflower   weed

Skill-Up

Recognizing the Five W's: The Five W's refer to the question words *who, when, what, where,* and *why.*

✭ Read the story again. Then, answer each question.

1 Who goes to the flower garden?

2 When does she go to the flower garden?

3 What flowers are there?

4 Where does the girl go?

5 Why does she go there?

Ready to Write

Ⓐ Read the story again and find the following.

1　Find every "is/are + -ed" and circle them.

2　Find every flower and underline them.

Ⓑ Look and write.

1　　(iris, plant)

　　》 *Some irises are planted.*

2　　(daisy, water)

　　》

3　(orchid, pick)

　　》

Read & Write

- **Read the play before you write.**

〈Setting〉 *The flowers in the garden are talking to each other.*

Tulip　　　: I was watered by Tracy last night. It was wonderful.

Rose　　　: All the weeds were pulled up this morning. I feel great now.

Daisy　　　: Some of my flowers were picked today. They are in a vase now.

Sunflower: I was planted last week. It's nice to meet you, everyone.

Narrator　: All the flowers in the flower garden are very cheerful.

A Look at the flower garden. What flowers can you see? What are the people doing in the flower garden?

B Now, write your own play. Then, read it to the class.

〈Setting〉 *The flowers in the garden are talking to each other.*

_____ : I was _____.

It was _____.

_____ : _____

_____

_____ : _____

_____

_____ : _____

_____

Narrator : _____

_____

Unique Trees ⊙ Track 30

Today, I learned about trees in science class.

Mr. Lee informed us about some interesting trees.

For example, pine trees are covered with

needle-shaped leaves.

They don't have any wide leaves.

Pine seeds are found in pine cones.

These seeds are used for cooking in some regions.

Do you Know?

Pine trees are called evergreens. They stay green all year long. Other trees lose their leaves in fall.

Talk & Read

▪ **Look at the pictures. What kinds of trees do you see?**

Rubber trees are even more unique.

People make scratches on their trunks, and then rubber

milk comes from them.

Natural rubber is made from this milk.

I think both trees are helpful in our lives.

— Eric Bobo

| Genre | Blog Entry |

People write blog entries about many topics. They often write about what they did during the day.

Vocabulary

◎ Track 31

needle

seed

pine cone

region

scratch

Read & Check

A **Choose the main topic.**

The story is about _____.

ⓐ science class

ⓑ pine trees

ⓒ unique trees

B **Choose the correct answers.**

1　Where did Eric learn about trees?

　　ⓐ in science class　　ⓑ in history class　　ⓒ in math class

2　What is made from rubber trees?

　　ⓐ pine cones　　　　ⓑ scratches　　　　ⓒ natural rubber

C **According to the passage, we can tell that…**

　　ⓐ pine seeds are not delicious.

　　ⓑ Mr. Lee is a science teacher.

　　ⓒ pine trees are more useful than rubber trees.

Identifying Words

1 This is a grain of a plant.

2 This is a part of a pine tree. It has pine seeds.

3 This is an area of land.

4 This is a sharp mark like a line.

5 This is a thin tool for sewing. One side is sharp, and the other side has a little hole.

scratch   seed   needle   pine cone   region

Skill-Up

Fact and Opinion: A fact is something that is true. An opinion is someone's idea or feeling.

✼ Read the passage again. Then, write F for fact or O for opinion for each sentence.

1 I think both trees are helpful in our lives.

2 Pine seeds are found in pine cones.

3 Pine trees are covered with needle-shaped leaves.

4 Rubber trees are even more unique.

5 Pine seeds are used for cooking in some regions.

Ready to Write

A **Read the passage again and find the following.**

1 Find every "with," "in," and "from" and circle them.

2 Find every type of tree and underline them.

B **Look and write.**

1

(apple tree, filled with, apples)

» *The apple trees are filled with apples.*

2

(maple tree, found in, Canada)

»

3

(cherry tree, covered with, cherry blossoms)

»

Read & Write

▪ **Read the report before you write.**

There are many kinds of trees in the world.

The chestnut trees are filled with chestnuts.

They taste great.

The dogwood trees are covered with beautiful flowers.

They look wonderful.

I think all of these trees are amazing.

A **Look at the trees. What is special about these trees? Choose three of them you want to write about.**

pine tree /
needle-shaped leaves

maple tree /
found in Canada

orange tree /
filled with oranges

cherry tree /
covered with cherry
blossoms

redwood /
found in the western
United States

apple tree /
filled with apples

B **Now, write your own report. Include your own opinion of each tree. Then, read it to the class.**

There are many kinds of trees in the world.

These trees are _____.

The _____ are _____.

_____

The _____ are _____.

_____

The _____ are _____.

_____

I think _____.

WRITING POINT 5

Past Participles

- You can make the past participle forms of regular verbs by adding **-ed** to them.

  ⓔ The garden is **visited** by Suzie.

  Some flowers are **watered**.

  The weeds are **pulled** up.

- The past participle forms of irregular verbs do not end with **-ed**. They have different endings.

  ⓔ Many flowers are **grown** in the garden.

  Maple trees are **found** in Canada.

  The balloons are **blown** up.

Check-up

1. Circle the past participles in the sentences. Then, write them on the lines.

1) Some seeds are planted in the ground.　＿＿＿＿＿＿＿＿＿＿＿＿

2) The pine trees are covered with needles.　＿＿＿＿＿＿＿＿＿＿＿＿

3) The class is taught by Mr. Taylor.　＿＿＿＿＿＿＿＿＿＿＿＿

4) The plants are eaten by animals.　＿＿＿＿＿＿＿＿＿＿＿＿

5) The weeds are pulled up by the gardener.　＿＿＿＿＿＿＿＿＿＿＿＿

6) Toby was born in Colombia.　＿＿＿＿＿＿＿＿＿＿＿＿

7) The garage is cleaned by Mike.　＿＿＿＿＿＿＿＿＿＿＿＿

2. Correct the mistakes in the underlined words. Then, rewrite the sentences on the lines.

1) Some flowers are <u>waterd</u> by her. ····▶ _____

2) Maple trees are <u>cover</u> with red leaves. ····▶ _____

3) The picnic is <u>enjoyd</u> by everyone. ····▶ _____

4) The weeds are <u>pull</u> up by Justin. ····▶ _____

5) Redwoods are <u>finded</u> in the United States. ····▶ _____

Make It Yours

1. Check page 85. Did you use past participles correctly?

☐ Yes   ☐ No

2. Correct the sentences in the box below. Then, match them with the right pictures.

> ⓐ The garden is visit by Paul.
> ⓑ The flowers are waterd by Claire.
> ⓒ The fruit tree is fill with fruit.

1)

2)

3)

Chapter **6**
Movies

Tap Your Background Knowledge

- **Look at the pictures and talk together.**

exciting

frightening

? **Topic:** Opinions about Movies

◉ Track 32

1 What was the last movie you saw?
2 What did you think of that movie?

comical

imaginative

moving

actor

actress

director

cameraman

? **Topic:** Movie World

◎ Track 33

1   Who is your favorite actor or actress?
2   Who do you think the most important
    person in movie-making is?

writer

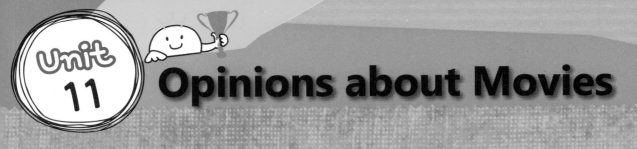

Unit 11 · Opinions about Movies

An Interview with Some Movie Fans ⊙ Track 34

Interviewer : Jake, tell me about the movie you saw last week.

Jake : I saw *The Dragon*. It was exciting because there were a lot of action scenes.

Interviewer : How about you, Lisa?

Lisa : I saw *Ghosts from the Past* last weekend. It was horrifying because the ghosts were really scary.

Do you Know?

There are people called movie critics. Their job is to write their opinions of movies.

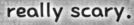

Talk & Read

- **Look at the picture. What are the children doing?**

Interviewer : What did you see Monique?

Monique : I saw *Last Ticket to L.A.* It wasn't great.

Interviewer : Why do you think so?

Monique : I disliked it because all the characters were very boring.

Bright School Broadcasting

Genre Interview

In an interview, a person asks one or more people questions about a topic. An interviewer asks questions, and an interviewee answers them.

Vocabulary Track 35

scene   horrifying   ghost   dislike   characters

Read & Check

A Choose the main topic.

The story is about _____.

ⓐ the most exciting new movies

ⓑ how Lisa enjoyed *Ghosts from the Past*

ⓒ the movies that three people saw

B Choose the correct answers.

1 What did Jake think of *The Dragon*?

    ⓐ It was horrifying.   ⓑ It was exciting.   ⓒ It was funny.

2 Why did Monique think the movie was NOT great?

    ⓐ The characters were boring.

    ⓑ The movie was scary.

    ⓒ The actors were not good.

C According to the story, we can tell that...

ⓐ Lisa never watches scary movies.

ⓑ Jake does not enjoy watching action movies.

ⓒ Monique will not recommend *Last Ticket to L.A.* to her friends.

Identifying Words

1 This means the same as "scary."

2 This is the spirit of a dead person.

3 These are the people or others appearing in a movie or book.

4 This is the opposite of "to like."

5 This is a small part of a movie, play, or book.

dislike   characters   scene   horrifying   ghost

Skill-Up

Identifying a Topic Sentence and Supporting Sentences:
The topic sentence tells you the main idea of the passage. The supporting sentences have detailed information about the topic.

☆ Read the story again. Then, fill in the blanks.

Topic Sentence   Tell me about the movie you saw last week.

Supporting Sentences

1 Jake: It was exciting because _____.

2 Lisa: It was horrifying because _____.

3 Monique: I disliked it because _____.

Ready to Write

A **Read the story again and find the following.**

1 Find every "because" and circle them.

2 Find every opinion about a movie and underline them.

B **Look and write.**

1  (frightening, many scary scenes)

» The movie was frightening because there were many scary scenes.

2 (comical, a lot of funny characters)

»

3 (exciting, many action scenes)

»

Read & Write

- **Read the movie review before you write.**

A Movie Review of *The First Alien*
By Paul Staunton

I saw *The First Alien*. It was about an alien on the Earth.
The alien met many people.
It was thrilling because the alien was interesting.
It was exciting because the actors were very good, too.
The last scene was moving because the music was really sad.
I think you should watch this movie.

A Look at the posters for each movie. Choose one of the movies you want to write about.

B Now, write your own movie review. Then, read it to the class.

A Movie Review of _____

By _____

I saw _____ .

_____

_____

It was _____ because _____ .

_____

It was _____ .

_____

_____

_____

_____

http://www.ray.com

A Message from Ray Savage

Track 36

Dear fans,

This is Ray Savage.

I have good news for you all.

I am going to start filming a new action movie soon.

Patty Taylor is going to act with me.

She is the main actress in the film.

We are going to shoot the movie in London, Egypt, and Mexico.

Do you Know?

Movie-making jobs include art director, casting director, editor, sound mixer, and composer.

Talk & Read

▪ **Look at the pictures. What are the people doing?**

Anna Wellman is going to direct the movie.

She wrote the story, too. I really liked the plot.

I can't wait to get started.

You are going to love this movie.

Wishing you the best,

Ray

Genre Website Post

A website post is a short message on a website. It can be a letter to people or a post with information in it.

Vocabulary

fans

act

shoot

film

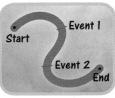
plot

Read & Check

A **Choose the main topic.**

The story is about _____.

ⓐ the life of Ray Savage

ⓑ a movie Ray Savage is going to film

ⓒ a film Ray Savage just saw

B **Choose the correct answers.**

1 Who is Patty Taylor?

ⓐ the main actress   ⓑ the director   ⓒ the main actor

2 Where will the movie NOT be filmed?

ⓐ Mexico   ⓑ France   ⓒ London

C **According to the passage, we can tell that...**

ⓐ Patty Taylor is from London.

ⓑ Ray Savage is excited about the movie.

ⓒ Ray Savage and Anna Wellman are friends.

Identifying Words

1 This means "to make a movie by using a camera."

2 This is another word for "movie."

3 This means "to perform."

4 These people like someone or something very much.

5 This means "the main story."

act   film   plot   fans   shoot

Skill-Up

Summarizing: Summarizing is making a long passage short. To write a good summary, readers need to find the important points of the passage.

✲ Fill in the blanks with the correct words in the word bank.

Ray Savage is going to film a new _____. _____ is going to be the main actress. They are going to _____ the movie in London, Egypt, and _____. Anna Wellman is going to _____ the movie. Ray Savage can't _____ to get started.

Word Bank

Patty Taylor   direct   shoot   Mexico   wait   movie

Ready to Write

A **Read the passage again and find the following.**

1   Find every "am/are/is + going to" and circle them.

2   Find every word after "going to" and underline them.

B **Look and write.**

1      (Chris Hunter, composer, write the soundtrack)

» Chris Hunter is a composer.

» He is going to write the soundtrack.

2   (Erika Lee, cameraman, film the movie)

»

»

3   (Mike Stewart, actor, act in the movie)

»

»

Read & Write

▪ **Look at the interview before you write.**

Interviewer	: What are you going to film next?
Mary Sheldon:	I'm going to film a comedy.
Interviewer	: Who is going to act in the movie?
Mary Sheldon:	Bruce Wright and I are going to act in it.
Interviewer	: When are you going to start it?
Mary Sheldon:	We are going to start it next month.

A Imagine you are a movie star. Fill in the blanks about your newest movie.

Type of Movie	Action Movie	Type of Movie	
Title of the Movie	Speed Boys	Title of the Movie	
Other Actor or Actress	Peter Clarkin	Other Actor or Actress	
Where You Are Filming	Paris	Where You Are Filming	
When You Will Start	next week	When You Will Start	

B Now, complete the interview. Use the information you wrote above to fill in the blanks.

Interviewer: What are you going to film next?

_____: I'm going to _____.

Interviewer: What is the title of the movie?

_____: _____

Interviewer: Who is going to act in the movie?

_____: _____

Interviewer: _____

_____: _____

Interviewer: _____

_____: _____

Interviewer: _____

_____: _____

WRITING POINT 6

Future Tense

> be verb + going to + verb

- Make the future tense by using "**am/are/is** + **going to** + **the base form of the verb**."

  ex I **am going to act** in a movie.

  They **are going to shoot** the movie in London.

  She **is going to direct** the movie.

- Use the future tense to talk about events that will happen at a later time.

  ex We **are going to have** a party next week.

  I **am going to** see him later today.

  Claire **is going to** meet us in a restaurant at 9.

Check-up

1. Circle the verbs that form the future tense in the sentences. Then, write the words on the lines.

1) I am going to see that movie tonight. _____

2) When are you going to go to the theater? _____

3) Patty is going to act in the movie. _____

4) The fans are going to love it. _____

5) We are going to study English next month. _____

6) She is going to visit Taiwan. _____

7) Sammy is going to start her concert soon. _____

2. Correct the mistakes in the underlined words. Then, rewrite the sentences on the lines.

1) I am going to <u>writing</u> a letter.

    ⋯▶ _____

2) He is <u>go</u> to act in an action movie next year.

    ⋯▶ _____

3) You are going to <u>liked</u> this horror movie.

    ⋯▶ _____

4) I am going to <u>buying</u> some popcorn tomorrow.

    ⋯▶ _____

Make It Yours

1. Check page 101. Did you use the future tense correctly?

◯ Yes   ◯ No

2. Correct the sentences in the box below. Then, match them with the right pictures.

ⓐ Jack is go to study tonight.

ⓑ They are going to having dinner.

ⓒ Ryan is going read books.

1)

2)

3)

WINNERS'
Reading & Writing
Workbook

Enjoy reading, then start writing with confidence!

5

Clue & Key

A Find and circle the words. Then, write them.

1 delicious digitalcamera dragon — **digital camera**

2 taxitrailtabletPCtabletraintruck

3 hippoheadphonesheadache

4 videovoicerecordervitaminviolin

B Read and choose the words that have the same meanings.

1 This is a special event. People sell old items at their homes.

ⓐ garage sale   ⓑ gadgets   ⓒ smartphone   ⓓ laptop

2 This is a computer. You can carry it with you.

ⓐ MP3 player   ⓑ TV   ⓒ laptop   ⓓ voice recorder

3 This is a cell phone. You can go online or watch video clips with it.

ⓐ TV   ⓑ laptop   ⓒ smartphone   ⓓ headphones

4 This machine can play music. You can carry it with you.

ⓐ TV   ⓑ MP3 player   ⓒ digital camera   ⓓ garage sale

C Write an "O" for the correct sentences and write an "X" for the wrong sentences.

1 This is Sara's laptop. This is his. **X**

2 This is my sister's MP3 player. This is hers. **O**

3 This is my voice recorder. This is mine. [ ]

4 This is Tom's TV. This is mine. [ ]

5 This is your laptop. This is yours. [ ]

6 It is your tablet PC. It is mine. [ ]

7 They are John's headphones. They are hers. [ ]

D Rewrite the sentences in C. If there are any mistakes, correct them.

1 This is Sara's laptop. This is hers.

2 This is my sister's MP3 player. This is hers.

3 _____

4 _____

5 _____

6 _____

7 _____

A Garage Sale

"Wow, look at all this ¹⁾_____," says Tommy.

"My ²⁾_____ is having a garage sale," answers Beth.

Tommy looks at some ³⁾_____.

"Is this ⁴⁾_____ brother's smartphone?"

"Yes, it's his. This is his ⁵⁾_____ smartphone."

Tommy picks up a ⁶⁾_____.

"Is ⁷⁾_____ your mother's laptop?"

"No, it isn't hers. It's my laptop. Do you ⁸⁾_____ it?"

"No thanks. But I want the MP3 ⁹⁾_____."

"That's ¹⁰⁾_____, too. You can have it for a cheap price."

Word Box

gadgets	your	want	family	laptop
stuff	mine	this	old	player

A Unscramble the words.

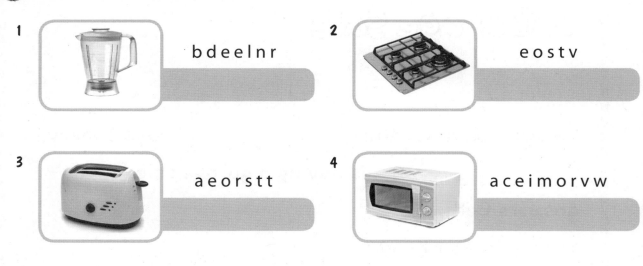

1 b d e e l n r

2 e o s t v

3 a e o r s t t

4 a c e i m o r v w

B Read and choose the words that have the same meanings.

1 This keeps food cold.

ⓐ toaster   ⓑ stove   ⓒ microwave   ⓓ refrigerator

2 This is cooked bread.

ⓐ toast   ⓑ toaster   ⓒ chop   ⓓ modern

3 This means "to cut something into small pieces."

ⓐ stove   ⓑ chop   ⓒ refrigerator   ⓓ toast

4 This is the opposite of "old."

ⓐ chop   ⓑ bread maker   ⓒ modern   ⓓ stove

5 This cooks food quickly.

ⓐ toaster   ⓑ refrigerator   ⓒ blender   ⓓ microwave

C Write an "O" for the correct sentences and write an "X" for the wrong sentences.

1 We are able to keep food cold in it. ☐

2 People are able cook food quickly in a microwave. ☐

3 We are able to make toast with a toaster. ☐

4 People able to cook food quickly. ☐

5 People are able freeze food with a freezer. ☐

6 We are able to make bread with a bread maker. ☐

7 People are able to chopping food with a blender. ☐

D Rewrite the sentences in C. If there are any mistakes, correct them.

1 _____

2 _____

3 _____

4 _____

5 _____

6 _____

7 _____

Technology in Our Kitchens

The modern [1]_____ has many machines.

They are [2]_____ to people.

[3]_____ kitchens have a refrigerator.

We are [4]_____ to keep food cold in it.

Most kitchens have a [5]_____ and a blender, too.

People are able to cook food [6]_____ in a microwave.

People are able to [7]_____ food with a blender.

[8]_____ kitchens have a toaster.

We are able to make toast [9]_____ a toaster.

They make [10]_____ very easy.

Word Box

Some	chop	quickly	cooking	Most
with	able	microwave	kitchen	useful

A Unscramble the words.

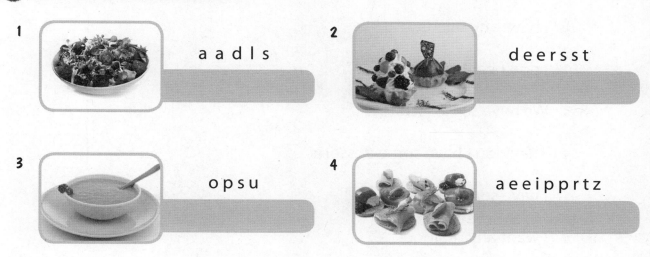

1   a a d l s

2   d e e r s s t

3   o p s u

4   a e e i p p r t z

B Read and choose the words that have the same meanings.

1   This food tastes like spaghetti. It has various shapes.

ⓐ iced tea   ⓑ waiter   ⓒ restaurant   ⓓ pasta

2   This person serves you at a restaurant.

ⓐ waiter   ⓑ order   ⓒ soup   ⓓ dessert

3   You can order food and eat at this place.

ⓐ dessert   ⓑ appetizer   ⓒ restaurant   ⓓ main dish

4   This is cold tea. It is usually served with ice.

ⓐ pasta   ⓑ soup   ⓒ salad   ⓓ iced tea

5   This is something you do at a restaurant to get food. You usually tell this
to the waiter.

ⓐ order   ⓑ iced tea   ⓒ appetizer   ⓓ soup

C Write an "O" for the correct sentences and write an "X" for the wrong sentences.

1 I have any salads. ☐

2 I don't have some pasta. ☐

3 We have some iced tea. ☐

4 They don't have some desserts. ☐

5 I have some soup. ☐

6 I want any seafood. ☐

7 We don't have any appetizers. ☐

D Rewrite the sentences in C. If there are any mistakes, correct them.

1 _____

2 _____

3 _____

4 _____

5 _____

6 _____

7 _____

A Night at a Restaurant

<Setting> A boy and a girl are having 1)_____

in a restaurant.

Waiter : May I 2)_____ your order, please?

Molly : Do you have any 3)_____?

Waiter: 4)_____, we have some salads.

Steve : Do you have any appetizers?

Waiter : Sorry. We don't have 5)_____ appetizers.
Today's specail is pasta. Do you want some?

Steve : Okay. I'll have some pasta, 6)_____.

Waiter : How about you, 7)_____? Do you
want some pasta, too?

Molly : [Thinking for a while] No thanks. I want some
salads and 8)_____.

Waiter: Sure. 9)_____ to drink?

Molly : We'd 10)_____ some iced tea, please.

Word Box

please	take	seafood	dinner	miss
any	salads	Yes	Anything	like

9

A Find and circle the words. Then, write them.

1  sunsoupsushiseafoodsteak

2  petplanepaellapinepeachpear

3  lemonlasagnaleathersouplap

4  favoritechocolatefishandchips

B Read and choose the words that have the same meanings.

1 This is a type of food like spaghetti and ramen.

ⓐ noodles　　ⓑ taco　　ⓒ sushi　　ⓓ paella

2 This is a Mexican food with meat, cheese, vegetables, and sauce in a hard shell.

ⓐ taco　　ⓑ travel　　ⓒ pad Thai　　ⓓ noodles

3 This means "to take a trip."

ⓐ travel　　ⓑ delicious　　ⓒ taco　　ⓓ noodles

4 This is another word for "tasty."

ⓐ delicious　　ⓑ pad Thai　　ⓒ sushi　　ⓓ travel

C Write an "O" for the correct sentences and write an "X" for the wrong sentences.

1 If you go to Russia, you should have stuffed cabbage. ☐

2 you go to India, you should have curry and naan. ☐

3 If you visit Thailand, you should eat pad Thai. ☐

4 you go to Spain you should eat paella. ☐

5 you visit England, you should have fish and chips. ☐

6 If you go to Mexico, you should have tacos. ☐

7 If you travel to Japan you should eat sushi and ramen. ☐

D Rewrite the sentences in C. If there are any mistakes, correct them.

1 _____

2 _____

3 _____

4 _____

5 _____

6 _____

7 _____

E **Listen and fill in the blanks by using the word box.** ⊙ Track 41

Special Foods for Your Travels

There are a lot of ¹⁾_____ foods in every country.

²⁾_____ you visit Thailand, you should eat pad Thai.

If you travel to Japan, you ³⁾_____ eat sushi and ramen.

You ⁴⁾_____ love the noodles.

If you go to ⁵⁾_____, you should have tacos and salsa.

Tacos and salsa are ⁶⁾_____ but delicious.

If you ⁷⁾_____ England, you should try fish and ⁸⁾_____.

If you go to Spain, you should ⁹⁾_____ paella.

These foods will make your travels very ¹⁰⁾_____.

Word Box

chips	will	visit	should	have
Mexico	spicy	special	traditional	If

A **Find and circle the words. Then, write them.**

1

AugustAladdinAprilapple

2

Goldilocksgoldmedalgold

3

coffeecupsCinderellacake

4

pizzapianoPinocchiopeas

B **Read and choose the words that have the same meanings.**

1 This is another word for "smart."

ⓐ castle   ⓑ intelligent   ⓒ active   ⓓ witch

2 This means "busy and energetic."

ⓐ intelligent   ⓑ witch   ⓒ castle   ⓓ active

3 This is a woman. She can use bad magic.

ⓐ witch   ⓑ popular   ⓒ active   ⓓ castle

4 This means "well-liked."

ⓐ castle   ⓑ active   ⓒ intelligent   ⓓ popular

C Write an "O" for the correct sentences and write an "X" for the wrong sentences.

1　I am handsomer than you. ☐

2　Jamie is more active than Sue. ☐

3　He is most popular than her. ☐

4　My sister is more intelligent you. ☐

5　I am more beautiful than Cinderella. ☐

6　Snow White is popular than Gretel. ☐

7　Paul is more friendly than Ryan. ☐

D Rewrite the sentences in C. If there are any mistakes, correct them.

1 _____

2 _____

3 _____

4 _____

5 _____

6 _____

7 _____

14

A Party at the Castle

Some fairy tale women are having a 1)_____ at the castle.

"I'm more active 2)_____ you. I can swim everywhere," 3)_____ the Little Mermaid.

"But I'm more intelligent than you," 4)_____ Gretel.

"I tricked the 5)_____ witch.

"I'm more 6)_____," says Snow White.

"Prince Charming loves me."

"But my 7)_____ are more expensive than yours," says Little Red Riding Hood.

"Look at my 8)_____ red clothes."

"I'm 9)_____ than everyone," says Sleeping Beauty. "I'm going to 10)_____ now."

Word Box

bed	evil	says	than	answers
clothes	sleepier	party	nice	popular

A Find and circle the words. Then, write them.

1

bestboatBatmanbeaverbed

2

woodweedwiperWoodywet

3

supermarketsunshineSuperman

4

OctoberoctopusOptimusPrime

B Read and choose the words that have the same meanings.

1 This is a superhero's ability such as flying in the sky.

ⓐ lazy ⓑ superpower ⓒ peaceful ⓓ imaginary

2 This means "quiet and restful."

ⓐ scary-looking ⓑ peaceful ⓒ lazy ⓓ superpower

3 This is the opposite of "actual" or "real."

ⓐ imaginary ⓑ peaceful ⓒ lazy ⓓ superpower

4 This means "slow to move and react."

ⓐ peaceful ⓑ lazy ⓒ superpower ⓓ scary-looking

C Write an "O" for the correct sentences and write an "X" for the wrong sentences.

1 Superman likes flying in the sky. ☐

2 Shrek likes help others. ☐

3 I enjoy studying English. ☐

4 My brother likes play the piano. ☐

5 He really enjoys use kung fu for others. ☐

6 Some people like watch movies. ☐

7 I like helping people in trouble. ☐

D Rewrite the sentences in C. If there are any mistakes, correct them.

1 _____

2 _____

3 _____

4 _____

5 _____

6 _____

7 _____

Famous Movie Characters

by Carla Waters

There are many famous movie 1)_____.

Shrek is a 2)_____ ogre.

Ogres are imaginary 3)_____. They like fighting.

But Shrek 4)_____ living a peaceful life.

Panda Po in *Kung Fu Panda* is an animal character.

Pandas are 5)_____ slow and lazy.

But Panda Po is very 6)_____. He enjoys doing

kung fu.

Spiderman is a 7)_____.

8)_____ walls is his superpower.

Those are some of people's 9)_____ movie

characters.

They are all 10)_____.

But all of them love helping weak people.

Word Box

| scary-looking | energetic | different | monsters | superhero |
| enjoys | Climbing | characters | usually | favorite |

A Unscramble the words.

1   u y f n n

2   g n o r s t

3   a e m n

4   a m r s t

B Read and choose the words that have the same meanings.

1   This person is very good at sports.

   ⓐ Earth   ⓑ smart   ⓒ athlete   ⓓ merchant

2   This means "having a feeling of wanting more and more."

   ⓐ Earth   ⓑ smart   ⓒ servant   ⓓ greedy

3   This person buys and sells goods and earns money.

   ⓐ greedy   ⓑ palace   ⓒ merchant   ⓓ athlete

4   This is our planet.

   ⓐ palace   ⓑ announce   ⓒ Earth   ⓓ servant

5   This is a king's or queen's home.

   ⓐ servant   ⓑ palace   ⓒ Earth   ⓓ greedy

C Write an "O" for the correct sentences and write an "X" for the wrong sentences.

1 Gemma is strongest girl in my class. ☐

2 He is silliest boy. ☐

3 My sister is the cutest. ☐

4 I am the tallest person in the world. ☐

5 Claire has the longst hair. ☐

6 Sam has the bigest feet in my family. ☐

7 Dan is the smartest. ☐

D Rewrite the sentences in C. If there are any mistakes, correct them.

1 _____

2 _____

3 _____

4 _____

5 _____

6 _____

7 _____

A Greedy King

One day, a king announces, "I want the [1]_____ people."

Two weeks later, many people [2]_____ the palace.

"I'm the [3]_____ athlete," says a man.

"I'm the [4]_____ witch," says a woman.

"I'm the [5]_____ merchant," says another man.

"And I'm the [6]_____ person," says a boy.

The king says, "I'm the [7]_____ king on Earth.

You cannot go [8]_____ to your homes.

All of you should work for me [9]_____."

"What?" say the people.

"You're so [10]_____. Goodbye."

Word Box

greedy	best	happiest	richest	back
tallest	visit	smartest	forever	funniest

A Find and circle the words. Then, write them.

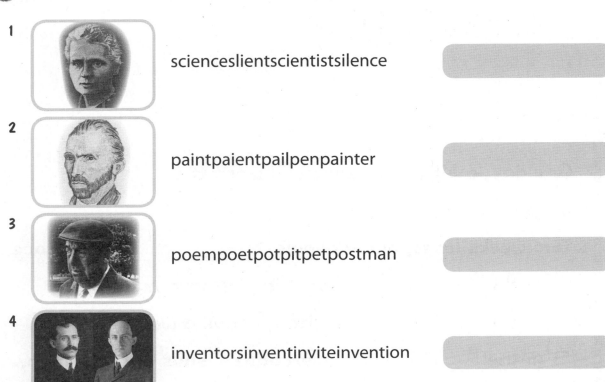

1 scienceslientscientistsilence

2 paintpaientpailpenpainter

3 poempoetpotpitpetpostman

4 inventorsinventinviteinvention

B Read and choose the words that have the same meanings.

1 This is the opposite of "to forget."

ⓐ wife ⓑ general ⓒ remember ⓓ president

2 This is a woman. She is married to her husband.

ⓐ hardworking ⓑ president ⓒ general ⓓ wife

3 This is the leader of a country.

ⓐ president ⓑ wife ⓒ hardworking ⓓ remember

4 This is the opposite of "lazy."

ⓐ remember ⓑ general ⓒ hardworking ⓓ president

C Write an "O" for the correct sentences and write an "X" for the wrong sentences.

1   When he was 30, he travels around the world.   ☐

2   When she was 55, she became the president.   ☐

3   When I am 35, I got married.   ☐

4   When she was 10, she moved to London.   ☐

5   In 1809, Abraham Lincoln is born.   ☐

6   When he was 32, he wrote his first play.   ☐

7   When she was 22, she studied law.   ☐

D Rewrite the sentences in C. If there are any mistakes, correct them.

1   _____

2   _____

3   _____

4   _____

5   _____

6   _____

7   _____

George Washington

George Washington was a great man in American
1) _____.

He 2) _____ up in Virginia.

He was an 3) _____ and hardworking child.

When he 4) _____ 21, he joined the army.

When he was 27, he 5) _____ married.

His 6) _____ was Martha Custis.

When he was 43, he became a 7) _____ in the
army.

When he was 57, he became the 8) _____
president 9) _____ the United States.

In 1799, he died, but a lot of people still
10) _____ him.

Word Box

of	honest	history	got	first
wife	grew	was	general	remember

Chapter 5

Unit 09 Flowers

A Unscramble the words.

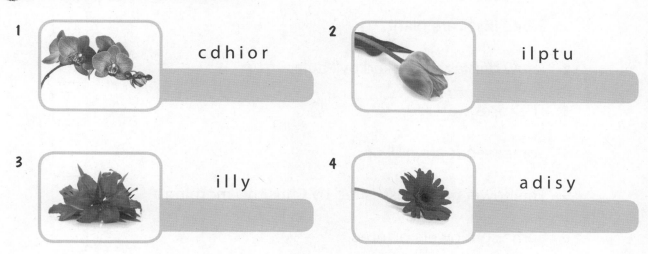

1 c d h i o r

2 i l p t u

3 i l l y

4 a d i s y

B Read and choose the words that have the same meanings.

1 This is an outdoor place with many flowers.

ⓐ sunflower   ⓑ weed   ⓒ water   ⓓ flower garden

2 This is a bad plant in a flower garden.

ⓐ weed   ⓑ daisy   ⓒ sunflower   ⓓ water

3 This means "to remove from the ground."

ⓐ flower garden   ⓑ pull up   ⓒ water   ⓓ sunflower

4 This means "to give flowers water."

ⓐ water   ⓑ rose   ⓒ weed   ⓓ pull up

5 This is a tall yellow flower.

ⓐ weed   ⓑ sunflower   ⓒ water   ⓓ pull up

C Write an "O" for the correct sentences and write an "X" for the wrong sentences.

1　Some irises are plant. ☐

2　A few daisies are picked by Paula. ☐

3　The roses watered. ☐

4　Some weeds are pull up. ☐

5　The flower garden is visited by Chris this morning. ☐

6　Some sunflowers planted. ☐

7　The lilies are water by her. ☐

D Rewrite the sentences in C. If there are any mistakes, correct them.

1 _____

2 _____

3 _____

4 _____

5 _____

6 _____

7 _____

Listen and fill in the blanks by using the word box. ⦿Track 46

In the Garden

Suzie ¹⁾_____ her flower garden in the morning.

She goes there to have a great time.

She waters ²⁾_____ roses.

She ³⁾_____ up some weeds around the tulips.

She picks a ⁴⁾_____ daisies, and then she plants

some sunflowers.

Suzie has a ⁵⁾_____ garden.

The flower ⁶⁾_____ is visited by Suzie in the

morning.

The roses are ⁷⁾_____.

Some weeds around the tulips are pulled ⁸⁾_____.

A few daisies are picked, and then some ⁹⁾_____

are planted.

¹⁰⁾_____ a nice garden Suzie has!

Word Box

up	visits	her	garden	sunflowers
wonderful	watered	pulls	few	What

A Find and circle the words. Then, write them.

1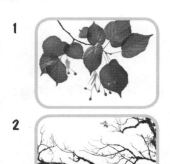

leaveleafleftleaveslives

2

breakbrokebrandbranches

3

fruitsflutefriedfrogflutes

4

bootsrightrootsroopes

B Read and choose the words that have the same meanings.

1 This is a part of a pine tree. It has pine seeds.

   ⓐ needle   ⓑ seed   ⓒ pine cone   ⓓ scratch

2 This is a grain of a plant.

   ⓐ seed   ⓑ region   ⓒ scratch   ⓓ needle

3 This is a sharp mark like a line.

   ⓐ region   ⓑ pine cone   ⓒ needle   ⓓ scratch

4 This is an area of land.

   ⓐ pine cone   ⓑ needle   ⓒ seed   ⓓ region

C Write an "O" for the correct sentences and write an "X" for the wrong sentences.

1 Redwoods are found with the western United States. ☐

2 Natural rubber is made from rubber milk. ☐

3 The orange trees filled with oranges. ☐

4 The pine trees are covered with needles. ☐

5 Pine seeds are found by pine cones. ☐

6 Rubber trees are found with Thailand. ☐

7 The apple trees are filled with apples. ☐

D Rewrite the sentences in C. If there are any mistakes, correct them.

1 _____

2 _____

3 _____

4 _____

5 _____

6 _____

7 _____

Unique Trees

Today, I learned about trees in 1)_____ class.

Mr. Lee 2)_____ us about some interesting trees.

For 3)_____, pine trees are covered with needle-shaped leaves.

They don't have any wide 4)_____.

Pine 5)_____ are found in pine cones.

These seeds are 6)_____ for cooking in some regions.

Rubber trees are even more 7)_____.

People make scratches on their 8)_____, and then rubber milk comes from them.

Natural rubber is 9)_____ from this milk.

I think both trees are 10)_____ in our lives.

– Eric Bobo

Word Box

example	helpful	trunks	seeds	unique
leaves	science	informed	made	used

Chapter 6

Unit 11 Opinions about Movies

A Unscramble the words.

1 *Escape to Fairyland*   a a e g i i i m n t v

2 *Binky the Clown*   a c c i l m o

3 *A Mother's Tale*   g i m n o v

4 *Race To The Moon*   c e g i i n t x

B Read and choose the words that have the same meanings.

1 This means the same as "scary."

ⓐ ghost   ⓑ horrifying   ⓒ scene   ⓓ comical

2 This is the opposite of "to like."

ⓐ dislike   ⓑ boring   ⓒ ghost   ⓓ horrifying

3 This is a small part of a movie, play, or book.

ⓐ scene   ⓑ ghost   ⓒ comical   ⓓ dislike

4 This is the spirit of a dead person.

ⓐ horrifying   ⓑ dislike   ⓒ scene   ⓓ ghost

5 These are the people or others appearing in a movie or book.

ⓐ ghost   ⓑ characters   ⓒ dislike   ⓓ scene

C Write an "O" for the correct sentences and write an "X" for the wrong sentences.

1. It was frightening because there were many scary scenes. ☐

2. *Shrek* comical because it was very funny. ☐

3. The movie was boring while the music was bad. ☐

4. It exciting because there were a lot of action scenes. ☐

5. It horrifying because the ghosts were really scary. ☐

6. It was comical because there were a lot of funny characters. ☐

7. I disliked the movie if all the characters were boring. ☐

D Rewrite the sentences in C. If there are any mistakes, correct them.

1 _____

2 _____

3 _____

4 _____

5 _____

6 _____

7 _____

Listen and fill in the blanks by using the word box. ⊚ Track 48

An Interview with Some Movie Fans

Interviewer : Jake, 1)_____ me about the movie
you saw last week.

Jake : I saw *The Dragon*.
It was exciting 2)_____ there were
a lot of action 3)_____.

Interviewer : How 4)_____ you, Lisa?

Lisa : I saw *Ghosts from the Past* last weekend.
It was 5)_____ because the ghosts
were really 6)_____.

Interviewer : What 7)_____ you see Monique?

Monique : I saw *Last Ticket to L.A.* It wasn't great.

Interviewer : Why do you 8)_____ so?

Monique : I 9)_____ it because all the
characters were very 10)_____.

Word Box

scary	scenes	disliked	did	horrifying
because	about	tell	boring	think

A Find and circle the words. Then, write them.

1

actionaccentactorappleantair

2

directiondictionarydirectordune

3

digitalcameracamelcameraman

4

waiterwaterwriterwestcoastwet

B Read and choose the words that have the same meanings.

1 This means "to make a movie by using a camera."

   ⓐ act   ⓑ fan   ⓒ shoot   ⓓ script

2 This is another word for "movie."

   ⓐ film   ⓑ shoot   ⓒ actress   ⓓ fan

3 This means "to perform."

   ⓐ fan   ⓑ script   ⓒ act   ⓓ film

4 These people like someone or something very much.

   ⓐ actor   ⓑ writer   ⓒ fans   ⓓ script

C Write an "O" for the correct sentences and write an "X" for the wrong sentences.

1   She is going act with me.   ☐

2   They are going to shoot the movie in Paris.   ☐

3   Jack is going to directed the movie.   ☐

4   I am going write the soundtrack.   ☐

5   Eric Simpson is going direct the movie.   ☐

6   We are going to shoot the movie next month.   ☐

7   They are going to starting the new film soon.   ☐

D Rewrite the sentences in C. If there are any mistakes, correct them.

1   _____

2   _____

3   _____

4   _____

5   _____

6   _____

7   _____

A Message from Ray Savage

Dear 1)_____,

2)_____ is Ray Savage.

I have good 3)_____ for you all.

I am going to start filming a new action movie soon.

Patty Taylor is going to 4)_____ with me.

She is the 5)_____ actress in the film.

We are going to 6)_____ the movie in London,

Egypt, and Mexico.

Anna Wellman is going to 7)_____ the movie.

She wrote the story, too. I really liked the 8)_____.

I can't wait to get 9)_____.

You are going to love this movie.

10)_____ you the best,

Ray

Word Box

Wishing	act	plot	started	This
main	fans	shoot	direct	news

36

Winners' Reading & Writing is a seven-book course specially designed for learners of English from beginner to intermediate level. It has been developed to help learners dramatically improve both their reading and writing skills. Learners will experience stories covering a number of genres that are both interesting and informative. Following this, learners will be able to create a concrete piece of writing which will incorporate the target patterns. *Winners' Reading & Writing* will allow all English learners to develop the ability to read freely and to write with greater confidence.

Features

- Organized guides to every stage of reading and writing
- Providing a number of vocabulary categorized by various themes
- Introducing diverse genres with fun and educational stories
- Dealing with core grammar patterns for ESL/EFL learners
- Writing Point sections with sufficient exercises to develop accurate writing

Components

Student Book / Workbook

Downloadable Resources at http://www.clueandkey.com

WINNERS' Reading & Writing Series

- WINNERS' Reading & Writing STARTER
- WINNERS' Reading & Writing ❶
- WINNERS' Reading & Writing ❷
- WINNERS' Reading & Writing ❸
- WINNERS' Reading & Writing ❹
- WINNERS' Reading & Writing ❺
- WINNERS' Reading & Writing ❻